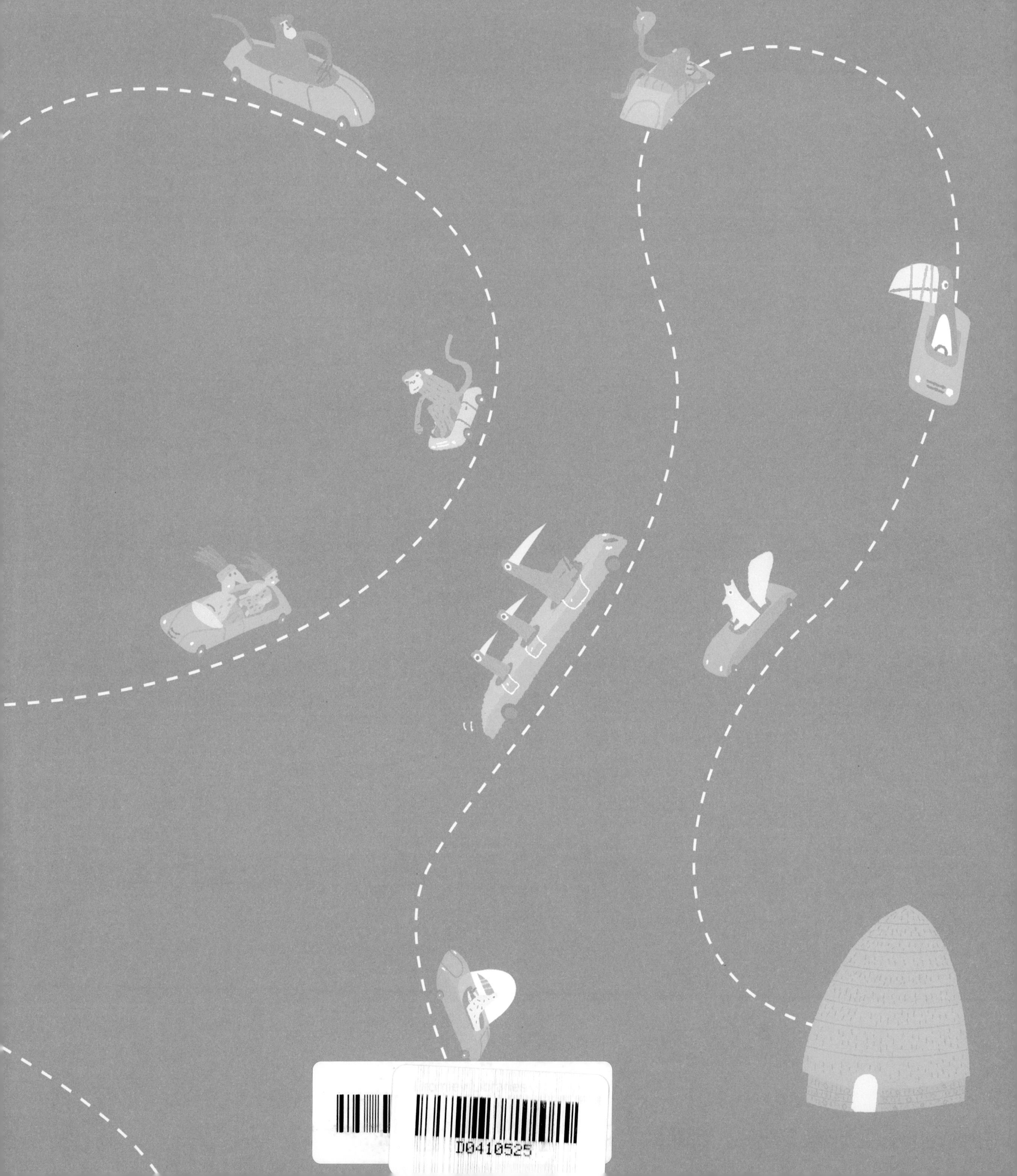

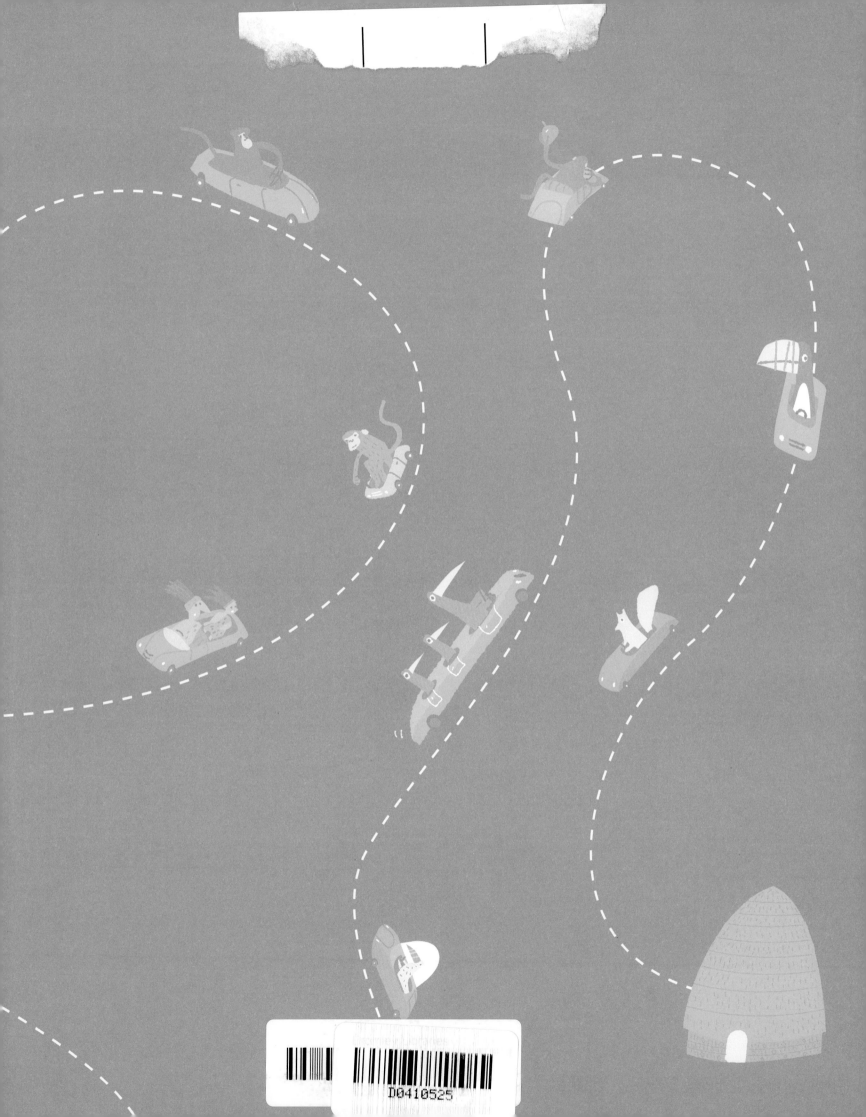

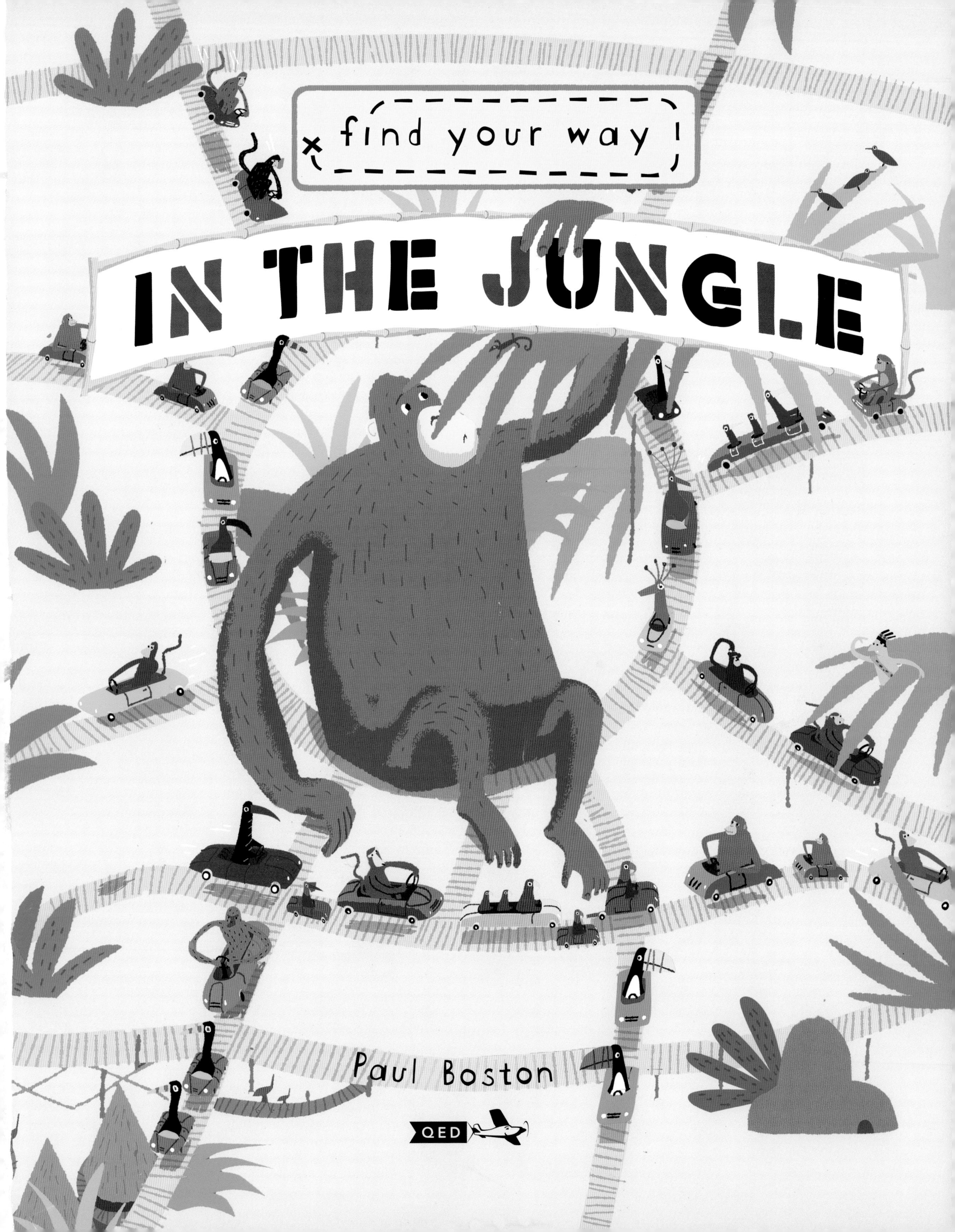
find your way
IN THE JUNGLE
Paul Boston
QED

YOUR MISSION

We are the Leafies. We are putting on a festival to celebrate the king's birthday. Find your way to the festival tent by choosing which exits or entrances to follow on each page.

1 Choose your transport

Tuk-tuk

Elephant

Capybara

2 Trace a route

There are lots to choose from and you can go **BACKWARDS** and **FORWARDS** along the same road.

3 Collect on every page

Choose **ONE** of the missions below to help the Leafies. You will find one of each object in every scene.

Collect **12 RED FEATHERS** to make a headdress for the king.

Collect **12 BLUE BANANAS** to make a special punch.

Collect **12 YELLOW KAZOOS** for the band members.

4

Use the book LIKE A REAL MAP

Turn the pages and use co-ordinates in this book just like you would with a real map. You can find out more about co-ordinates on pages 4 and 5.

5

SOLVE maths puzzles

Along the way you will come across Leafies who are lost or need your help. You will have to use your super maths skills to help them. You might be asked to count up to ten or to find a shape.

Welcome to the jungle

Look at the map of the jungle. Can you see where the festival tent is? It has lots of coloured flags. That's where you need to get to. Let's use co-ordinates to help us describe where the festival tent is on the map.

What are co-ordinates?

Co-ordinates are a set of letters and numbers that show where something is on a map. The letter comes first, followed by the number, so the festival tent is in (D, 1). Look for the co-ordinate symbol throughout the book.

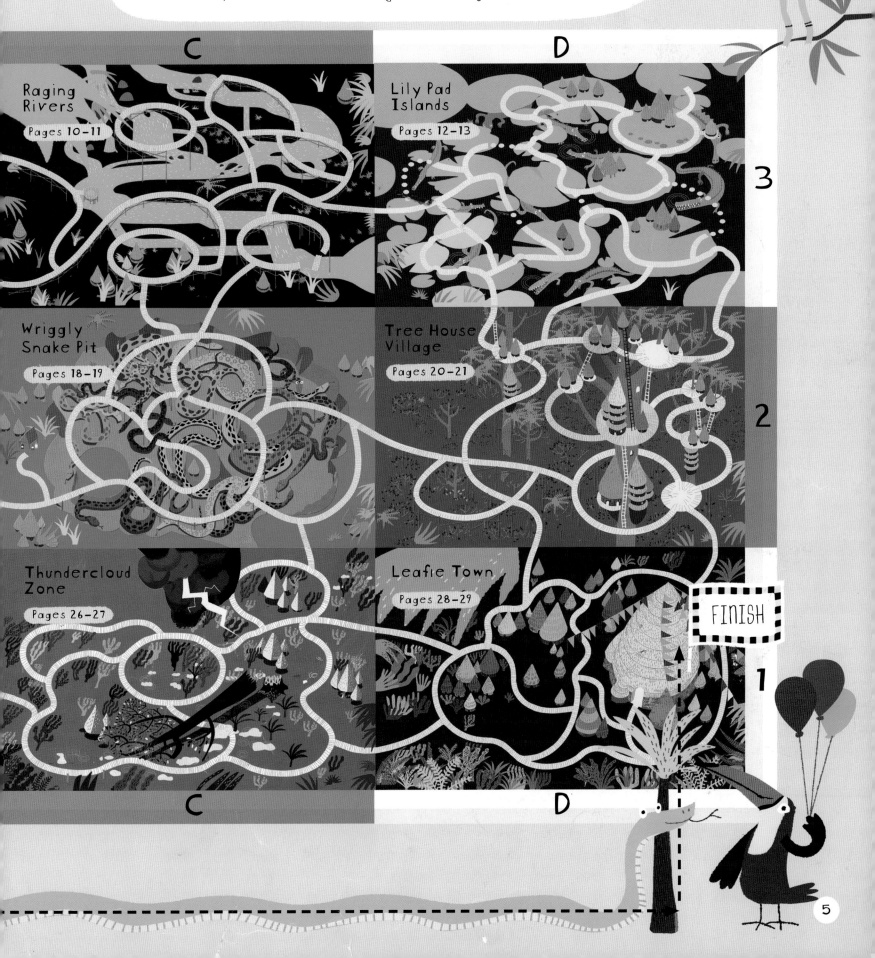

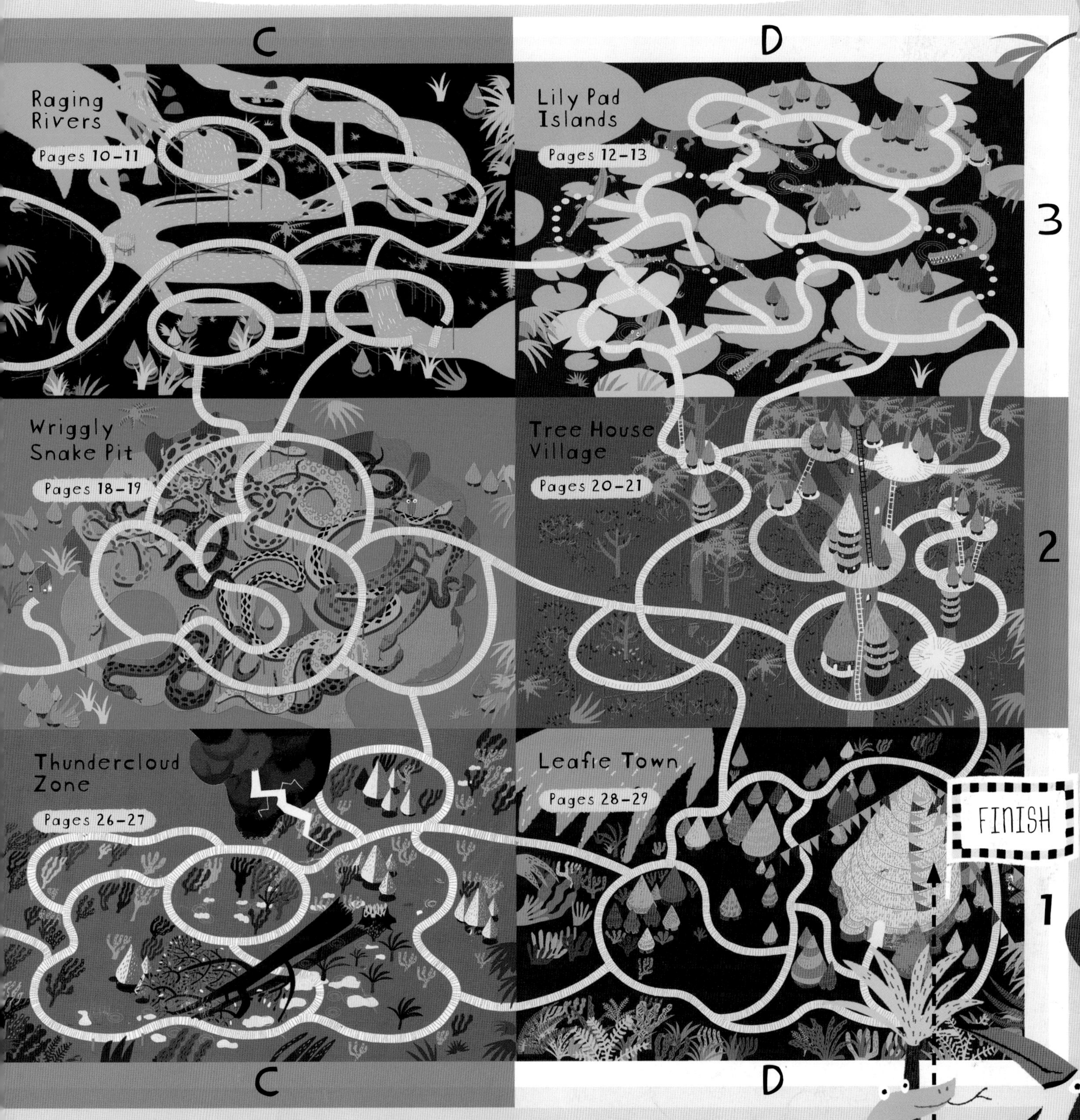

Oh dear! Precious the orangutan is sitting in the middle of the roundabout! She is too big to move so you will have to go around her in order to find your object.
RED FEATHER
BLUE BANANA
YELLOW KAZOO
A
B
C
3
2
1
FRUIT
How many pink cars can you count?
CAMPING SHOP
Who lives in the hut with three windows?
ORANGUTAN JUNCTION
START HERE
Can you tell me the co-ordinates for the camping shop?
Go to page 14
TEMPLE RUINS

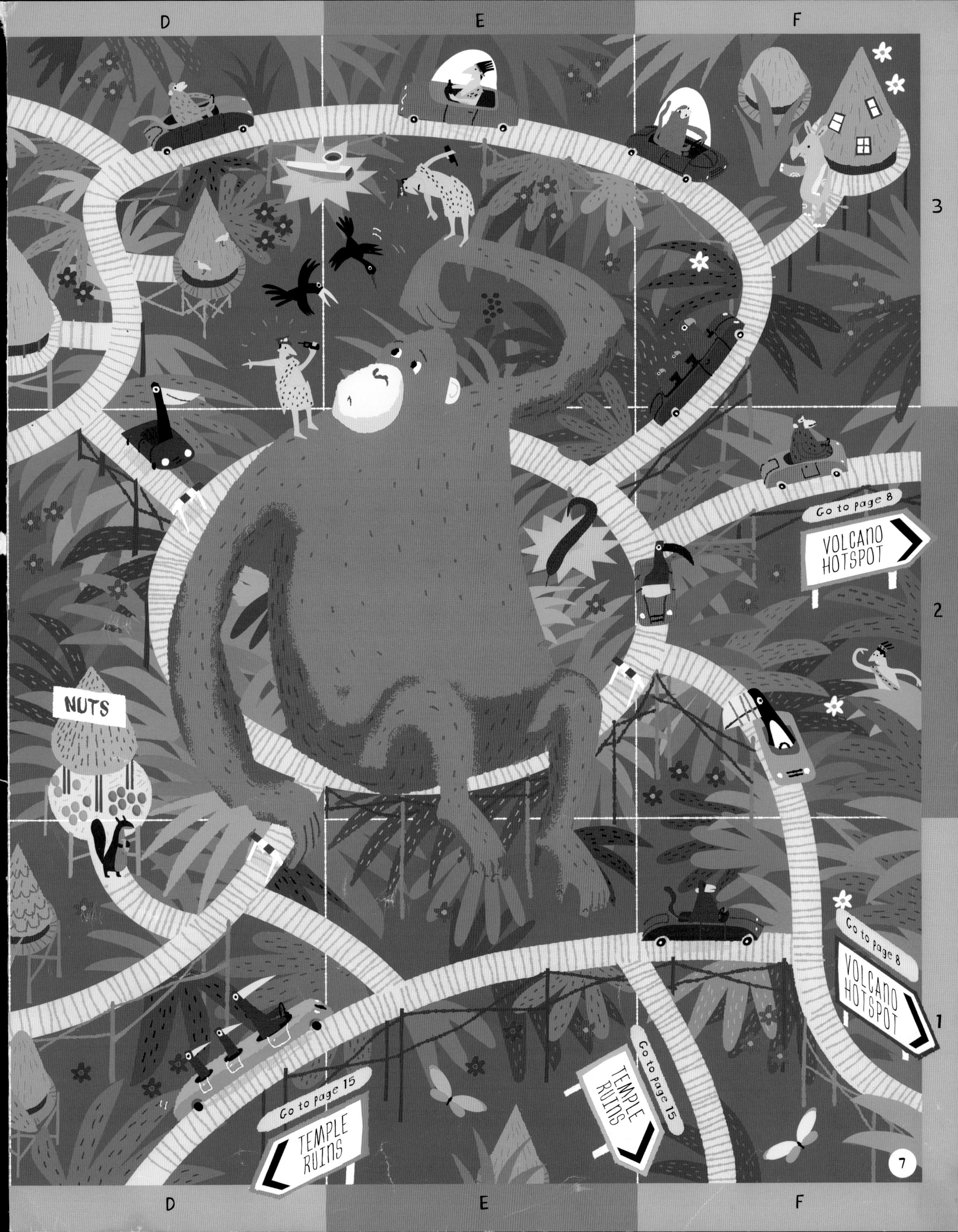
D
E
F
3
2
1
Go to page 8
VOLCANO HOTSPOT
Go to page 8
VOLCANO HOTSPOT
NUTS
Go to page 15
TEMPLE RUINS
Go to page 15
TEMPLE RUINS
D
E
F

Look out! That volcano is about to erupt. The animals who live here need to wear heatproof suits. To travel through safely and find your object, use any of the tunnels you can find.

RED FEATHER

BLUE BANANA

YELLOW KAZOO

D
E
F
Which pizza has a quarter missing?
HOT PIZZA
3
Go to page 10
RAGING RIVERS
I'm lost! Is the jewellery hut in (D,2) or (C,1)?
JEWELLERY HUT
2
BUBBLY BATHS
Go to page 10
RAGING RIVERS
1
Go to page 17
DIAMOND CAVE
D
E
F

Hold on tight! The water flows quickly here and the bridges are slippery. Watch out for snapping piranhas, too - they might try and eat your object!

RED FEATHER

BLUE BANANA

YELLOW KAZOO

D
E
F
Are there more pink dolphins or yellow canoes in the river?
CANOE HIRE
3
2
Go to page 12
LILY PAD ISLANDS
Help, I'm lost! Can you tell me where to find the pink dolphin lookout?
1
Go to page 19
WRIGGLY SNAKE PIT
D
E
F

A
B
C
3
2
1
What's this? The water is much calmer here, but it's covered in giant lily pads! In places, you will need to hop from one lily pad to the next, but try not to step on a crocodile's head!
RED FEATHER
BLUE BANANA
YELLOW KAZOO
How many turtles can you count in the water?
LILY PAD ISLANDS
Go to page 11
RAGING RIVERS
Where can I buy some coffee?
Go to page 20
TREE HOUSE VILLAGE
A
B
C

D
E
F
3
2
1
COFFEE HUTS
CROCODILE FOOD
Use the stepping stones to cross safely here. Count aloud as you cross.
CHOCOLATE ISLAND
Go to page 21
TREE HOUSE VILLAGE
Go to page 21
TREE HOUSE VILLAGE
D
E
F

You've reached the temple ruins!

A great king used to live here thousands of years ago. The temple is now overrun by monkeys and tree roots. Watch your step as you collect your object.

RED FEATHER

BLUE BANANA

YELLOW KAZOO

D
E
F
Go to page 7
ORANGUTAN JUNCTION
3
How many purple monkeys can you count? Which one is upside down?
2
Go to page 16
DIAMOND CAVE
Go to page 16
DIAMOND CAVE
1
Go to page 23
SMELLY PLANT PATCH
D
E
F

Uh oh, it's gone dark!

You've entered the diamond cave. Are those sparkling diamonds or watching eyes shining in the cave walls? Grab your torch and watch out for the train that passes through!

RED FEATHER
BLUE BANANA
YELLOW KAZOO

D
E
F
Go to page 9
VOLCANO HOTSPOT
3
Which co-ordinates is the heart-shaped diamond in?
2
How many cars have their lights on?
Go to page 18
WRIGGLY SNAKE PIT
1
Go to page 25
SPROUTING SAPLINGS
D
E
F

Yikes! You've entered the snake pit. Try not to get in a tangle as you search for your object. Luckily, the snakes are sleeping, but be careful, don't wake them up!

RED FEATHER

BLUE BANANA

YELLOW KAZOO

D
E
F
Go to page 11
RAGING RIVERS
Which snake has a diamond-shaped pattern?
3
Go to page 20
TREE HOUSE VILLAGE
2
Oh no! Which snake is awake?
1
Go to page 27
THUNDERCLOUD ZONE
D
E
F

Ah, civilisation at last!

This wonderful tree village is where the Leafies live. Don't look down as their houses are high in the treetops. Tread carefully as you collect your object.

RED FEATHER

BLUE BANANA

YELLOW KAZOO

D
E
F
Go to page 13
LILY PAD ISLANDS
TREETOP CAFE
FOREST SCHOOL
FUEL
Go to page 29
LEAFIE TOWN
3
2
1
D
E
F

Phew! That dreadful smell is coming from the red rafflesia plant. It smells like rotten meat to attract flies. Put a clothes peg on your nose before you go near it, or you might faint!

RED FEATHER

BLUE BANANA

YELLOW KAZOO

D
E
F
Go to page 15
TEMPLE RUINS
CLOTHES PEGS
Go to page 24
SPROUTING SAPLINGS
3
Collect your clothes pegs from (B,1) or (F,3)!
Go to page 24
SPROUTING SAPLINGS
2
Venus Flytrap
1
D
E
F

How sad. All the trees in this part of the jungle have been cut down. Luckily, there are many workers here who are planting new ones. Can you help them on your way?

RED FEATHER BLUE BANANA YELLOW KAZOO

D
E
F
Go to page 17
DIAMOND CAVE
3
Can you tell me where the Tree Store is? I want to collect some seeds.
WATERING CANS
Go to page 26
THUNDERCLOUD ZONE
2
1
Which plant has grown two little flowers?
D
E
F

Oh no! Head undercover quickly, a tropical monsoon has started! Lightning has split a huge tree in two and it is now blocking the road. Travel around it carefully to continue your mission.

RED FEATHER

BLUE BANANA

YELLOW KAZOO

D
E
F
Go to page 19
WRIGGLY SNAKE PIT
HOT DRINKS
COATS
Go to page 28
LEAFIE TOWN
Who is hiding under the smallest palm tree?
Go to page 28
LEAFIE TOWN
3
2
1
D
E
F

Yipee! You've made it to Leafie Town. Can you see the festival tent where the birthday celebrations are taking place? Make your way over and don't forget to pick up your remaining object as you go.

RED FEATHER

BLUE BANANA

YELLOW KAZOO

D
E
F
Go to page 21
TREE HOUSE VILLAGE
3
CAKES
I'm ready to party! To enter the tent, turn the page...
FESTIVAL TENT
2
BALLOONS
1
D
E
F

Well done! You have completed your mission and reached the Festival Tent. This is a great birthday party! Can you see where you need to put your twelve objects? What else can you see? Join in the celebrations!
Are there more balloons than presents?
Happy birthday to you!
The band are ready to start. But four of the players are dancing! Can you find them and give them your kazoos? They are wearing purple badges.
Please bring your red feathers over here! The headdress is almost finished.

The special punch is almost ready! Please add your blue bananas to the top of the fountain.
How many cups on the table are empty?
Which is the tallest cake? I'm going to eat it all!
Can you spot the jelly that is shaped like a pyramid?

MORE JUNGLE FUN!

Understanding Co-ordinates

Encourage your child to look at other places where they might find co-ordinates, such as on an A-Z map. Draw a pirate's map together and plan your route to the treasure! Perhaps it's buried deep in the jungle or on a beach.

Counting

Go back through the book and look for more opportunities to encourage counting in the jungle. How many spots does the snake have? How many piranhas are in the river?

Telling the Time

Play the game 'Feeding Time at the Zoo'. Make a list of all the jungle animals you can think of. Start by writing the time next to the first animal in the list, and then fill in the chart by writing lots of statements. For example, 'The elephants need to be fed one hour after the giraffes', or 'The tigers and monkeys need feeding at the same time'.

Recognising Shapes

Make a giraffe! Cut out lots of different 2D shapes from coloured paper. You could use a rectangle for the long neck, a square for the body and hexagons for the spots. You could even try using 3D shapes from plasticine or cardboard tubes.

Maths Problems and Vocabulary

Go back through the book and look for opportunities to build on mathematic vocabulary and problem solving skills. For example, if there are five flowers with six petals each, how many petals are there altogether? Are there more animals driving blue cars than red cars?

Measurements

Go on a scavenger hunt! Write a checklist of items to collect including; the longest twig, the widest leaf, the thinnest blade of grass and the biggest stone.

Quarto Knows

Quarto is the authority on a wide range of topics.
Quarto educates, entertains and enriches the lives of our readers—enthusiasts and lovers of hands-on living.
www.quartoknows.com

Written and edited by: Joanna McInerney and the QED team
Designed by: Mike Henson
Consultant: Alistair Bryce-Clegg

First published in the UK in 2016 by
QED Publishing
Part of The Quarto Group
The Old Brewery, 6 Blundell Street,
London, N7 9BH

A catalogue record for this book is available from the British Library.

ISBN 978 1 78493 633 4

Printed in China